Mysterious Wonders of Antiquity

By
Manly P. Hall

Copyright © 2022 Lamp of Trismegistus. All rights reserved. No part of this publication may be reproduced or transmitted in any form or by any means, electronic or mechanical, including photocopying, recording, or by any information storage and retrieval system, without permission in writing from Lamp of Trismegistus. Reviewers may quote brief passages.

ISBN: 978-1-63118-598-4

Esoteric Classics

Other Books in this Series and Related Titles

Aurora of the Philosophers by Paracelsus (978-1-63118-507-6)

Rosicrucian Rules, Secret Signs, Codes and Symbols by various (978-1-63118-488-8)

On the Philadelphian Gold by Philochrysus & Philadelphus (978-1-63118-511-3)

Paracelsus, the Four Elements and Their Spirits by M P Hall (978-1-63118-400-0)

The Stone of the Philosophers by A E Waite (978-1-63118-509-0)

Freher's Process in the Philosophical Work by D A Freher (978-1-63118-484-0)

The Rosicrucian Chemical Marriage by Christian Rosenkreuz (978-1-63118-458-1)

The Alchemical Catechism of Paracelsus by Paracelsus (978-1-63118-513-7)

Alchemy in the Nineteenth Century by Helena P. Blavatsky (978-1-63118-446-8)

Rosicrucians and Speculative Masonry in the Seventeenth Century (978-1-63118-489-5)

Qabbalistic Teachings and the Tree of Life by M P Hall (978-1-63118-482-6)

The Sepher Yetzirah and the Qabalah by M P Hall (978-1-63118-481-9)

The Devil in Love by Jacques Cazotte (978–1–63118–499–4)

Fortune-Telling with Dice by Astra Cielo (978-1-63118-466-6)

History, Analysis and Secret Tradition of the Tarot by Hall &c (978-1-63118-445-1)

Crystal Vision Through Crystal Gazing by Frater Achad (978-1-63118-455-0)

The Golden Verses of Pythagoras: Five Translations (978-1-63118-479-6)

Arcane Formulas or Mental Alchemy by W W Atkinson (978-1-63118-459-8)

The Machinery of the Mind by Dion Fortune (978-1-63118-451-2)

The A E Waite Reader: A Selection of Occult Essays (978-1-63118-515-1)

The Leadbeater Reader: A Selection of Occult Essays (978-1-63118-483-3)

Audio versions are also available on Audible, Amazon and Apple

Other Books in this Series and Related Titles

Ancient Mysteries and Secret Societies by Manly P Hall (978–1–63118–597–7)

The Zodiac and Its Signs by Manly P Hall (978–1–63118–596–0)

Life and Teachings of Hermes Trismegistus by Manly P Hall (978–1–63118–595–3)

The Secrets of Doctor Taverner by Dion Fortune (978–1–63118–594–6)

Vegetarianism, Theosophy & Occultism by Leadbeater &c (978–1–63118–593–9)

Applied Theosophy by Henry S Olcott (978–1–63118–592–2)

Higher Consciousness by C W Leadbeater (978–1–63118–591–5)

Theories About Reincarnation and Spirits by H P Blavatsky (978–1–63118–590–8)

The Use and Power of Thought by C W Leadbeater (978–1–63118–589–2)

Commentary on the Pymander by G R S Mead (978–1–63118–588–5)

Hypnotism and Mesmerism by Annie Besant (978–1–63118–587–8)

Spirits of Various Kinds by Helena P Blavatsky (978–1–63118–586–1)

The Hidden Language of Symbolism by Annie Besant (978–1–63118–585–4)

Eastern Magic & Western Spiritualism by Henry S Olcott (978–1–63118–584–7)

Spiritual Progress and Practical Occultism by H P Blavatsky (978–1–63118–583–0)

Memory and Consciousness by Besant & Blavatsky (978–1–63118–582–3)

The Origin of Evil by Helena P Blavatsky (978–1–63118–581–6)

The Camp of Philosophy: Studies in Alchemy by Bloomfield (978–1–63118–580–9)

The Testaments of the Twelve Patriarchs (978–1–63118–579–3)

Occult or Exact Science? by Helena P Blavatsky (978–1–63118–578–6)

Occultism, Semi-Occultism & Pseudo Occultism by A Besant (978–1–63118–577–9)

Audio versions are also available on Audible, Amazon and Apple

Table of Contents

Introduction...7

Wonders of Antiquity...9

The Greek Oracles...17

Seven Wonders of the World...29

INTRODUCTION

The word "esoteric" can be difficult to define. Esotericism in general can be seen less as a system of beliefs and more as a category, which encompasses numerous, different systems of beliefs. It's a bit of juxtaposition, since the word "esoteric" indicates something that few people know about, while the term itself broadly covers numerous philosophies, practices, areas of study and belief systems.

In a greater sense, Esotericism acts as a storehouse for secret knowledge, which is often considered ancient (by *tradition, if not by fact*), passed down from generation to generation, in private. At various times in history, simply possessing the knowledge of some of these subjects, was considered illegal and a jailable offence, if discovered. This usually included such general topics as Alchemy, Pharmacology, Qabalah, Hermeticism, Occultism, Ceremonial Magic, Astrology, Divination, Rosicrucianism and so on. Collectively, these areas of study were often referred to as the esoteric sciences.

Sometimes, the outer garment of a subject isn't esoteric, while what is hidden beneath it, is. As an example, Freemasonry isn't necessarily esoteric by nature (at *least not anymore*), but certain signs, passwords and handshakes given to the candidate during their initiation, are in fact, esoteric, in the sense that they are hidden from the general public.

Today, in the twenty-first century, such topics are readily available at bookstores across the country, and numerous main-steam publishers offer beginners guides and coffee-table volumes on many of these subjects, intended for mass appeal. Books like *"The Secret"* have turned previously arcane topics into household knowledge. All that being the case, however, it isn't to say that there still aren't buried secrets to uncover, ancient wisdom being ignored and forgotten mysteries to be explored. In fact, it is often that we are only able to further our own studies by standing on the shoulders of these disappearing giants.

Lamp of Trismegistus is doing its part to help preserve humanity's esoteric history by making some of these classics available to those students who are seeking to unearth the knowledge of these ancient colossi.

So, be sure to check other titles from our *Esoteric Classics* series, as well as our *Occult Fiction, Theosophical Classics, Foundations of Freemasonry Series, Supernatural Fiction, Paranormal Research Series, Studies in Buddhism* and our *Christian Apocrypha Series*. You can also download the audio versions of most of these titles from Amazon, Apple or Audible, for learning on the go.

WONDERS OF ANTIQUITY

IT was a common practice among the early Egyptians, Greeks, and Romans to seal lighted lamps in the sepulchers of their dead as offerings to the God of Death. Possibly it was also believed that the deceased could use these lights in finding his way through the Valley of the Shadow. Later as the custom became generally established, not only actual lamps but miniatures of them in terra cotta were buried with the dead. Some of the lamps were enclosed in circular vessels for protection; and instances have been recorded in which the original oil was found in them, in a perfect state of preservation, after more than 2,000 years. There is ample proof that many of these lamps were burning when the sepulchers were sealed, and it has been declared that they were still burning when the vaults were opened hundreds of years later. The possibility of preparing a fuel which would renew itself as rapidly as it was consumed has been a source of considerable controversy among mediæval authors. After due consideration of the evidence at hand, it seems well within the range of possibility that the ancient priest-chemists did manufacture lamps that burned, if not indefinitely, at least for considerable periods of time.

Numerous authorities have written on the subject of ever-burning lamps. W. Wynn Westcott estimates the number of writers who have given the subject consideration as more than 150, and H. P. Blavatsky as 173. While conclusions reached by different authors are at variance, a majority admit the existence of these phenomenal lamps. Only a few maintained that the lamps would burn forever, but many were willing to concede that they might remain alight for several centuries without replenishment of the fuel. Some considered the so-called perpetual lights as mere artifices of the crafty pagan priests, while a great many, admitting that the lamps actually burned, made the sweeping assertion that the Devil was using this apparent miracle to ensnare the credulous and thereby lead their souls to perdition.

On this subject the learned Jesuit, Athanasius Kircher, usually dependable, exhibits a striking inconsistency. In his *Œdipus Ægyptiacus* he writes: "Not a few of these ever-burning lamps have been found to be the devices of devils, * * * And I take it that all the lamps found in the tombs of the Gentiles dedicated to the worship of certain gods, were of this kind, not because they burned, or have been reported to burn, with a perpetual flame, but because probably the devil set them there, maliciously intending thereby to obtain fresh credence for a false worship."

Having admitted that dependable authorities defend the existence of the ever-burning lamps, and that even the Devil lends himself to their manufacture, Kircher next declared the entire theory to be desperate and impossible, and to be classed with perpetual motion and the Philosopher's Stone. Having already solved the problem to his satisfaction once, Kircher solves it again--but differently--in the following words: "In Egypt there are rich deposits of asphalt and petroleum. What did these clever fellows [the priests] do, then, but connect an oil deposit by a secret duct with one or more lamps, provided with wicks of asbestos! How could such lamps help burning perpetually? * * * In my opinion this is the solution of the riddle of the supernatural everlastingness of these ancient lamps."

Montfaucon, in his *Antiquities*, agrees in the main with the later deductions of Kircher, believing the fabled perpetual lamps of the temples to be cunning mechanical contrivances. He further adds that the belief that lamps burned indefinitely in tombs was the result of the noteworthy fact that in some cases fumes resembling smoke poured forth from the entrances of newly opened vaults. Parties going in later and discovering lamps scattered about the floor assumed that they were the source of the fumes.

There are several interesting stories concerning the discoveries of ever-burning lamps in various parts of the world. In a tomb on the Appian Way which was opened during the papacy of Paul III was found a burning lamp which had remained alight in a hermetically sealed vault for nearly 1,600 years. According to an account written by a contemporary, a body--that of a young and beautiful girl with long golden hair--was found floating in an unknown transparent liquid and as well preserved as though death had occurred but a few hours before. About the interior of the vault were a number of significant objects, which included several lamps, one of them alight. Those entering the sepulcher declared that the draft caused by the opening of the door blew out the light and the lamp could not be relighted. Kircher reproduces an epitaph, "TULLIOLAE FILIAE MEAE," supposedly found in the tomb, but which Montfaucon declares never existed, the latter adding that although conclusive evidence was not found, the body was generally believed to be that of Tulliola, the daughter of Cicero.

Ever-burning lamps have been discovered in all parts of the world. Not only the Mediterranean countries but also India, Tibet, China, and South America have contributed records of lights which burned continuously without fuel. The examples which follow were selected at random from the imposing list of perpetual lamps found in different ages.

Plutarch wrote of a lamp that burned over the door of a temple to Jupiter Ammon; the priests declared that it had remained alight for centuries without fuel.

St. Augustine described a perpetual lamp, guarded in a temple in Egypt sacred to Venus, which neither wind nor water could extinguish. He believed it to be the work of the Devil.

An ever-burning lamp was found at Edessa, or Antioch, during the reign of the Emperor Justinian. It was in a niche over the city gate, elaborately enclosed to protect it from the elements. The date upon it proved that the lamp had been burning for more than 500 years. It was destroyed by soldiers.

During the early Middle Ages a lamp was found in England which had burned since the third century after Christ. The monument containing it was believed to be the tomb of the father of Constantine the Great.

The Lantern of Pallas was discovered near Rome in A.D. 1401. It was found in the sepulcher of Pallas, son of Evander, immortalized by Virgil in his *Æneid*. The lamp was placed at the head of the body and had burned with a steady glow for more than 2,000 years.

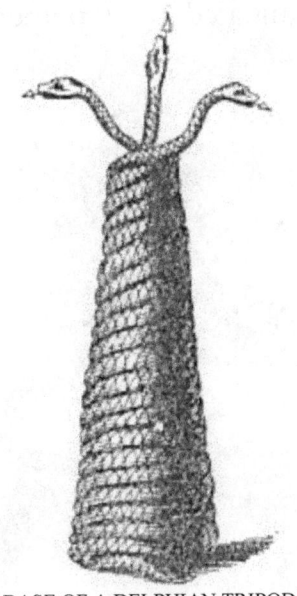

BASE OF A DELPHIAN TRIPOD[1]

In A.D. 1550 on the island of Nesis, in the Bay of Naples, a magnificent marble vault was opened in which was found a lamp still alight which had been placed there before the beginning of the Christian Era.

Pausanias described a beautiful golden lamp in the temple of Minerva which burned steadily for a year without refueling or having the wick trimmed. The ceremony of filling the lamp took place annually, and time was measured by the ceremony.

---

[1] From Montfaucon's *Antiquities*.

The windings of these serpents formed the base, and the three heads sustained the three feet of the tripod. It is impossible to secure satisfactory information concerning the shape and size of the celebrated Delphian tripod. Theories concerning it are based (in most part) upon small ornamental tripods discovered in various temples.

According to the *Fama Fraternitatis*, the crypt of Christian Rosencreutz when opened 120 years after his death was found to be brilliantly illuminated by a perpetual lamp suspended from the ceiling.

THE DELPHIAN TRIPOD RESTORED[2]

Numa Pompilius, King of Rome and magician of considerable power, caused a perpetual light to burn in the

---

[2] From Beaumont's *Gleanings of Antiquities*.

According to Beaumont, the above is the most authentic form of the Delphian tripod extant; but as the tripod must have changed considerably during the life of the oracle, hasty conclusions are unwise. In his description of the tripod, Beaumont divides it into four Parts: (1) a frame with three (2), a reverberating basin or bowl set in the frame; (e) a flat plate or table upon which the Pythia sat; and (4) a cone-shaped cover over the table, which completely concealed the priestess and from beneath which her voice sounded forth in weird and hollow tones, Attempts have been made to relate the Delphian tripod with the Jewish Ark of the Covenant. The frame of three legs was likened to the Ark of the Covenant; the flat plate or table to the Mercy Seat; and the cone-shaped covering to the tent of the Tabernacle itself. This entire conception differs widely from that popularly accepted, but discloses a valuable analogy between Jewish and Greek symbolism.

dome of a temple he had created in honor of an elemental being.

In England a curious tomb was found containing an automaton which moved when certain stones in the floor of the vault were stepped upon by an intruder. At that time the Rosicrucian controversy was at its height, so it was decided that the tomb was that of a Rosicrucian initiate. A countryman, discovering the tomb and entering, found the interior brilliantly lighted by a lamp hanging from the ceiling. As he walked, his weight depressed some of the floor stones. At once a seated figure in heavy armor began to move. Mechanically it rose to its feet and struck the lamp with an iron baton, completely destroying it, and thus effectually preventing the discovery of the secret substance which maintained the flame. How long the lamp had burned is unknown, but certainly it had been for a considerable number of years.

It is related that among the tombs near Memphis and in the Brahmin temples of India lights have been found in sealed chambers and vessels, but sudden exposure to the air has extinguished them and caused their fuel to evaporate.

It is now believed that the wicks of these perpetual lamps were made of braided or woven asbestos, called by the alchemists *salamander's wool*, and that the fuel was one of the products of alchemical research. Kircher attempted to extract oil from asbestos, being convinced that as the substance itself was indestructible by fire an oil extracted from it would supply the lamp with a fuel likewise indestructible. After spending two years in fruitless experimental work, he concluded that the task was impossible of accomplishment.

Several formulæ for the making of the fuel for the lamps have been preserved. In *Isis Unveiled*, H. P. Blavatsky reprints two of these formulæ from early authors--Tritenheim and Bartolomeo Korndorf. One will suffice to give a general understanding of the process:

"*Sulphur. Alum* ust. a ℥ iv.; sublime them into flowers to ℥ ij., of which add of crystalline Venetian borax (powdered) ℥ j.; upon these affuse high rectified spirit of wine and digest it, then abstract it and pour on fresh; repeat this so often till the sulphur melts like wax without any smoke, upon a hot plate of brass: this is for the *pabulum*, but the wick is to be prepared after this manner: gather the threads or thrums of the *Lapis asbestos*, to the thickness of your middle and the length of your little finger, then put them into a Venetian glass, and covering them over with the aforesaid depurated sulphur or aliment set the glass in sand for the space of twenty-four hours, so hot that the sulphur may bubble all the while. The wick being thus besmeared and anointed, is to be put into a glass like a scallop-shell, in such manner that some part of it may lie above the mass of prepared sulphur; then setting this glass upon hot sand, you must melt the sulphur, so that it may lay hold of the wick, and when it is lighted, it will burn with a perpetual flame and you may set this lamp in any place where you please."

THE GREEK ORACLES

The worship of Apollo included the establishment and maintenance of places of prophecy by means of which the gods could communicate with mankind and reveal futurity to such as deserved the boon. The early history of Greece abounds with accounts of talking trees, rivers, statues, and caves in which nymphs, dryads, or dæmons had taken up their abodes and from which they delivered oracles. While Christian authors have tried to prove that oracular revelations were delivered by the Devil for the purpose of misleading humanity, they have not dared to attack the theory of oracles, because of the repeated reference to it in their own sacred writings. If the onyx stones on the shoulders of Israel's high priest made known by their flashings the will of Jehovah, then a black dove, temporarily endowed with the faculty of speech, could indeed pronounce oracles in the temple of Jupiter Ammon. If the witch of Endor could invoke the shade of Samuel, who in turn gave prophecies to Saul, could not a priestess of Apollo call up the specter of her liege to foretell the destiny of Greece?

The most famous oracles of antiquity were those of Delphi, Dodona, Trophonius, and Latona, of which the talking oak trees of Dodona were the oldest. Though it is impossible to trace back to the genesis of the theory of oracular prophecy, it is known that many of the caves and fissures set aside by the Greeks as oracles were sacred long before the rise of Greek culture.

The oracle of Apollo at Delphi remains one of the unsolved mysteries of the ancients. Alexander Wilder derives the name *Delphi* from *delphos*, the womb. This name was chosen by the Greeks be cause of the shape of the cavern and the vent leading into the depths of the earth. The original name of the oracle was *Pytho*, so called because its chambers had been the abode of the great serpent *Python*, a fearsome creature that had crept out of the slime left by the receding flood that had destroyed all human beings except Deucalion and Pyrrha. Apollo, climbing the side of Mount Parnassus, slew the serpent after a prolonged combat, and threw the body down the fissure of the oracle. From that time the Sun God, surnamed the Pythian Apollo, gave oracles from the vent. With Dionysos he shared the honor of being the patron god of Delphi.

After being vanquished by Apollo, the spirit of Python remained at Delphi as the representative of his conqueror, and it was with the aid of his effluvium that the priestess was able to become *en rapport* with the god. The fumes rising from the fissure of the oracle were supposed to come from the decaying body of Python. The name *Pythoness*, or *Pythia*, given to the female hierophant of the oracle, means literally one who has been thrown into a religious frenzy by inhaling fumes rising from decomposing matter. It is of further interest to note that the Greeks believed the oracle of Delphi to be the umbilicus of the earth, thus proving that they considered the planet an immense human being. The connection between the principle of oracular revelation and the occult significance of the navel is an important secret belonging to the ancient Mysteries.

The oracle, however, is much older than the foregoing account indicates. A story of this kind was probably invented by the priests to explain the phenomena to those inquisitive persons whom they did not consider worthy of enlightenment regarding the true esoteric nature of the oracle. Some believe that the Delphic fissure was discovered by a Hypoborean priest, but as far back as recorded history goes the cave was sacred, and persons came from all parts of Greece and the surrounding countries to question the dæmon who dwelt in its chimney-like vent. Priests and priestesses guarded it closely and served the spirit who dwelt therein and who enlightened humanity through the gift of prophecy.

The story of the original discovery of the oracle is somewhat as follows: Shepherds tending their flocks on the side of Mount Parnassus were amazed at the peculiar antics of goats that wandered close to a great chasm on its southwestern spur. The animals jumped about as though trying to dance, and emitted strange cries unlike anything before heard. At last one of the shepherds, curious to learn the cause of the phenomenon, approached the vent, from which were rising noxious fumes. Immediately he was seized with a prophetic ecstasy; he danced with wild abandon, sang, jabbered inarticulate sounds, and foretold future events. Others went close to the fissure, with the same result. The fame of the place spread, and many came to learn of the future by inhaling the mephitic fumes, which exhilarated to the verge of delirium.

Some of those who came, being unable to control themselves, and having temporarily the strength of madmen, tore themselves from those seeking to restrain them, and, jumping into the vent, perished. In order to prevent others from doing likewise, a wall was erected around the fissure and a prophetess was appointed to act as mediator between the

THE PYTHIAN APOLLO[3]

oracle and those who came to question it. According to later authorities, a tripod of gold, ornamented with carvings of Apollo in the form of Python, the great serpent, was placed

---

[3] From *Historia Deorum Fatidicorum*.

Apollo, the twin brother of Diana, was the son of Jupiter and Latona. Apollo was fully adult at the time of his birth. He was considered to be the first physician and the inventor of music and song. The Greeks also acclaimed him to be father of the bow and arrow. The famous temple of Apollo at Delphi was rebuilt five times. The first temple was formed only of laurel branches; the second was somewhat similar; the third was brass and the fourth and fifth were probably of marble, of considerable size and great beauty. No other oracle in Greece equaled in magnificence that of Delphi in the zenith of its power. Writers declared that it contained many statues of solid gold and silver, marvelous ornaments, and implements of the most valuable materials and beautiful workmanship, donated by princes and kings who came from all parts of the civilized world to consult the spirit of Apollo dwelling in this sanctuary.

over the cleft, and on this was arranged a specially prepared seat, so constructed that a person would have difficulty in falling off while under the influence of the oracular fumes. just before this time, a story had been circulated that the fumes of the oracle arose from the decaying body of Python. It is possible that the oracle revealed its own origin.

For many centuries during its early history, virgin maidens were consecrated to the service of the oracle. They were called the *Phœbades*, or *Pythiæ*, and constituted that famous order now known as the Pythian priesthood. It is probable that women were chosen to receive the oracles because their sensitive and emotional nature responded more quickly and completely to "the fumes of enthusiasm." Three days before the time set to receive the communications from Apollo, the virgin priestess began the ceremony of purification. She bathed in the Castalian well, abstained from all food, drank only from the fountain of Cassotis, which was brought into the temple through concealed pipes, and just before mounting the tripod, she chewed a few leaves of the sacred bay tree. It has been said that the water was drugged to bring on distorted visions, or the priests of Delphi were able to manufacture an exhilarating and intoxicating gas, which they conducted by subterranean ducts and released into the shaft of the oracle several feet below the surface. Neither of these theories has been proved, however, nor does either in any way explain the accuracy of the predictions.

When the young prophetess had completed the process of purification, she was clothed in sanctified raiment and led to the tripod, upon which she seated herself, surrounded by the noxious vapors rising from the yawning fissure. Gradually, as she inhaled the fumes, a change came over her. It was as if a different spirit had entered her body. She struggled, tore her clothing, and uttered inarticulate cries. After a time her struggles ceased. Upon becoming calm a great majesty seemed to posses her, and with eyes fixed on space and body rigid, she uttered the prophetic words. The predictions were usually in the form of hexameter verse, but the words were often ambiguous and sometimes unintelligible. Every sound that she made, every motion of her body, was carefully recorded by the five Hosii, or holy men, who were appointed as scribes to preserve the minutest details of each divination. The Hosii were appointed for life, and were chosen from the direct descendants of Deucalion.

After the oracle was delivered, the Pythia began to struggle again, and the spirit released her. She was then carried or supported to a chamber of rest, where she remained till the nervous ecstasy had passed away.

Iamblichus, in his dissertation on *The Mysteries*, describes how the spirit of the oracle--a fiery dæmon, even Apollo himself--took control of the Pythoness and manifested through her: "But the prophetess in Delphi, whether she gives oracles to mankind through an attenuated and fiery spirit, bursting from the mouth of the cavern; or whether being seated in the adytum on a brazen tripod, or on a stool with four feet, she becomes sacred to the God; whichsoever of these is the case, she entirely gives herself up to a divine spirit, and is illuminated with a ray of divine fire. And when, indeed, fire ascending from the mouth of the cavern circularly invests her in collected abundance, she becomes filled from it with a divine splendour.

But when she places herself on the seat of the God, she becomes co-adapted to his stable prophetic power: and from both of these preparatory operations she becomes wholly possessed by the God. And then, indeed, he is present with and illuminates her in a separate manner, and is different from the fire, the spirit, the proper seat, and, in short, from all the visible apparatus of the place, whether physical or sacred."

Among the celebrities who visited the oracle of Delphi were the immortal Apollonius of Tyana and his disciple Damis. He made his offerings and, after being crowned with a laurel wreath and given a branch of the same plant to carry in his hand, he passed behind the statue of Apollo which stood before the entrance to the cave, and descended into the sacred place of the oracle. The priestess was also crowned with laurel and her head bound with a band of white wool. Apollonius asked the oracle if his name would be remembered by future generations. The Pythoness answered in the affirmative, but declared that it would always be calumniated. Apollonius left the cavern in anger, but time has proved the accuracy of the prediction, for the early church fathers perpetuated the name of Apollonius as the Antichrist. (For details of the story see *Histoire de la Magie*.)

The messages given by the virgin prophetess were turned over to the philosophers of the oracle, whose duty it was to interpret and apply them. The communications were then delivered to the poets, who immediately translated them into odes and lyrics, setting forth in exquisite form the statements supposedly made by Apollo and making them available for the populace.

Serpents were much in evidence at the oracle of Delphi. The base of the tripod upon which the Pythia sat was formed of the twisted bodies of three gigantic snakes. According to some authorities, one of the processes used to produce the prophetic ecstasy was to force the young priestess to gaze into the eyes of a serpent. Fascinated and hypnotized, she then spoke with the voice of the god.

Although the early Pythian priestesses were always maidens--some still in their teens--a law was later enacted that only women past fifty years of age should be the mouthpiece of the oracle. These older women dressed as young girls and went through the same ceremonial as the first Pythiæ. The change was probably the indirect result of a series of assaults made upon the persons of the priestesses by the profane.

During the early history of the Delphian oracle the god spoke only at each seventh birthday of Apollo. As time went on, however, the demand became so great that the Pythia was forced to seat herself upon the tripod every month. The times selected for the consultation and the questions to be asked were determined by lot or by vote of the inhabitants of Delphi.

It is generally admitted that the effect of the Delphian oracle upon Greek culture was profoundly constructive. James Gardner sums up its influence in the following words: "It responses revealed many a tyrant and foretold his fate. Through its means many an unhappy being was saved from destruction and many a perplexed mortal guided in the right way. It encouraged useful institutions, and promoted the progress of useful discoveries. Its moral influence was on the side of virtue, and its political influence in favor of the advancement of civil liberty." (See *The Faiths of The World*.)

The oracle of Dodona was presided over by Jupiter, who uttered prophecies through oak trees, birds, and vases of brass. Many writers have noted the similarities between the rituals of Dodona and those of the Druid priests of Britain and Gaul. The famous oracular dove of Dodona, alighting upon the branches of the sacred oaks, not only discoursed at length in the Greek tongue upon philosophy and religion, but also answered the queries of those who came from distant places to consult it.

The "talking" trees stood together, forming a sacred grove. When the priests desired answers to important questions, after careful and solemn purifications they retired to the grove. They then accosted the trees, beseeching a reply from the god who dwelt therein. When they had stated their questions, the trees spoke with the voices of human beings, revealing to the priests the desired information. Some assert that there was but one tree which spoke--an oak or a beech standing in the very heart of the ancient grove. Because Jupiter was believed to inhabit this tree he was sometimes called *Phegonæus*, or one who lives in a beech tree.

Most curious of the oracles of Dodona were the "talking" vases, or kettles. These were made of brass and so carefully fashioned that when struck they gave off sound for hours. Some writers have described a row of these vases and have declared that if one of them was struck its vibrations would be communicated to all the others and a terrifying din ensue.

Other authors describe a large single vase, standing upon a pillar, near which stood another column, supporting the statue of a child holding a whip. At the end of the whip were a number

THE DODONEAN JUPITER[4]

of swinging cords tipped with small metal balls, and the wind, which blew incessantly through the open building, caused the balls to strike against the vase. The number and intensity of the impacts and the reverberations of the vase were all carefully noted, and the priests delivered their oracles accordingly.

---

[4] From *Historia Deorum Fatidicorum*.

Jupiter was called Dodonean after the city of Dodona in Epirus. Near this city was a hill thickly covered with oak trees which from the most ancient times had been sacred to Jupiter. The grove was further venerated because dryads, fauns, satyrs, and nymphs were believed to dwell in its depths. From the ancient oaks and beeches were hung many chains of tiny bronze bells which tinkled day and night as the wind swayed the branches. Some assert that the celebrated talking dove of Dodona was in reality a woman, because in Thessaly both prophetesses and doves were called Peleiadas. It is supposed that the first temple of Dodona was erected by Deucalion and those who survived the great flood with him. For this reason the oracle at Dodona was considered the oldest in Greece.

When the original priests of Dodona--the *Selloi*--mysteriously vanished, the oracle was served for many centuries by three priestesses who interpreted the vases and at midnight interrogated the sacred trees. The patrons of the oracles were expected to bring offerings and to make contributions.

Another remarkable oracle was the Cave of Trophonius, which stood upon the side of a hill with an entrance so small that it seemed impossible for a human being to enter. After the consultant had made his offering at the statue of Trophonius and had donned the sanctified garments, he climbed the hill to the cave, carrying in one hand a cake of honey. Sitting down at the edge of the opening, he lowered his feet into the cavern. Thereupon his entire body was precipitately drawn into the cave, which was described by those who had entered it as having only the dimensions of a fair-sized oven. When the oracle had completed its revelation, the consultant, usually delirious, was forcibly ejected from the cave, feet foremost.

Near the cave of the oracle two fountains bubbled out of the earth within a few feet of each other. Those about to enter the cave drank first from these fountains, the waters of which seemed to possess peculiar occult properties. The first contained the water of forgetfulness, and all who drank thereof forgot their earthly sorrows. From the second fountain flowed the sacred water of Mnemosyne, or remembrance, for later it enabled those who partook of it to recall their experiences while in the cave.

Though its entrance was marked by two brass obelisks, the cave, surrounded by a wall of white stones and concealed in the heart of a grove of sacred trees, did not present an imposing appearance. There is no doubt that those entering it passed through strange experiences, for they were obliged to leave at the adjacent temple a complete account of what they saw and heard while in the oracle. The prophecies were given in the form of dreams and visions, and were accompanied by severe pains in the head; some never completely recovered from the after effects of their delirium. The confused recital of their experiences was interpreted by the priests according to the question to be answered. While the priests probably used some unknown herb to produce the dreams or visions of the cavern, their skill in interpreting them bordered on the Supernatural. Before consulting the oracle, it was necessary to offer a ram to the dæmon of the cave, and the priest decided by hieromancy whether the time chosen was propitious and the sacrifice was satisfactory.

THE SEVEN WONDERS OF THE WORLD

Many of the sculptors and architects of the ancient world were initiates of the Mysteries, particularly the Eleusinian rites. Since the dawn of time, the truers of stone and the hewers of wood have constituted a divinely overshadowed caste. As civilization spread slowly over the earth, cities were built and deserted; monuments were erected to heroes at present unknown; temples were built to gods who lie broken in the dust of the nations they inspired. Research has proved not only that the builders of these cities and monuments and the sculptors who chiseled out the inscrutable faces of the gods were masters of their crafts, but that in the world today there are none to equal them. The profound knowledge of mathematics and astronomy embodied in ancient architecture, and the equally profound knowledge of anatomy revealed in Greek statuary, prove that the fashioners of both were master minds, deeply cultured in the wisdom which constituted the arcana of the Mysteries .Thus was established the Guild of the Builders, progenitors of modern Freemasons. When employed to build palaces, temples or combs, or to carve statues for the wealthy, those initiated architects and artists concealed in their works the secret doctrine, so that now, long after their bones have returned to dust, the world realizes that those first artisans were indeed duly initiated and worthy to receive the wages of Master Masons.

The Seven Wonders of the World, while apparently designed for divers reasons, were really monuments erected to perpetuate the arcana of the Mysteries. They were symbolic structures, placed in peculiar spots, and the real purpose of their erection can be sensed only by the initiated. Eliphas Levi has noted the marked correspondence between these Seven Wonders and the seven planets. The Seven Wonders of the

TROPHONIUS OF LEBADIA[5]

---

[5] from *Historia Deorum Fatidicorum*.

Trophonius and his brother Agamedes were famous architects. While building a certain treasure vault, they contrived to leave one stone movable so that they might secretly enter and steal the valuables stored there. A trap was set by the owner, who had discovered the plot, and Agamedes was caught. To prevent discovery, Trophonius decapitated his brother and fled, hotly pursued. He hid in the grove of Lebadia, where the earth opened and swallowed him up. The spirit of Trophonius thereafter delivered oracles in the grove and its caverns. The name Trophonius means "to be agitated, excited, or roiled." It was declared that the terrible experiences through which consultants passed in the oracular caverns so affected them that they never smiled again. The bees which accompany the figure of Trophonius were sacred because they led the first envoys from Bœtia to the site of the oracle. The figure above is said

World were built by Widow's sons in honor of the seven planetary genii. Their secret symbolism is identical with that of the seven seals of Revelation and the seven churches of Asia.

1. The Colossus of Rhodes, a gigantic brass statue about 109 feet in height and requiring over twelve years to build, was the work of an initiated artist, Chares of Lindus. The popular theory--accepted for several hundred years--that the figure stood with one foot on each side of the entrance to the harbor of Rhodes and that full-rigged ships passed between its feet, has never been substantiated. Unfortunately, the figure remained standing but fifty-six years, being thrown down by an earthquake in 224 B.C. The shattered parts of the Colossus lay scattered about the ground for more than 900 years, when they were finally sold to a Jewish merchant, who carried the metal away on the backs of 700 camels. Some believed that the brass was converted into munitions and others that it was made into drainage pipes. This gigantic gilded figure, with its crown of solar rays and its upraised torch, signified occultly the glorious Sun Man of the Mysteries, the Universal Savior.

2. The architect Ctesiphon, in the fifth century B.C., submitted to the Ionian cities a plan for erecting a joint monument to their patron goddess, Diana. The place chosen was Ephesus, a city south of Smyrna. The building was constructed of marble. The roof was supported by 127 columns, each 60 feet high and weighing over 150 tons. The temple was destroyed by black magic about 356 B.C., but the world fixes the odious crime upon the tool by means of which

---

to be a production of a statue of Trophonius which was placed on the brow of the hill above the oracle and surrounded with sharply pointed stakes that it could not be touched.

the destruction was accomplished--a mentally deranged man named Herostratus. It was later rebuilt, but the symbolism was lost. The original temple, designed as a miniature of the universe, was dedicated to the moon, the occult symbol of generation.

3. Upon his exile from Athens, Phidias--the greatest of all the Greek sculptors--went to Olympia in the province of Elis and there designed his colossal statue of Zeus, chief of the gods of Greece. There is not even an accurate description of this masterpiece now in existence; only a few old coins give an inadequate idea of its general appearance. The body of the god was overlaid with ivory and the robes were of beaten gold. In one hand he is supposed to have held a globe supporting a figure of the Goddess of Victory, in the other a scepter surmounted by an eagle. The head of Zeus was archaic, heavily bearded, and crowned with an olive wreath. The statue was seated upon an elaborately decorated throne. As its name implies, the monument was dedicated to the spirit of the planet Jupiter,--one of the seven Logi who bow before the Lord of the Sun.

4. Eliphas Levi includes the Temple of Solomon among the Seven Wonders of the World, giving it the place occupied by the Pharos, or Lighthouse, of Alexandria. The Pharos, named for the island upon which it stood, was designed and constructed by Sostratus of Cnidus during the reign of Ptolemy (283-247 B.C.). It is described as being of white marble and over 600 feet high. Even in that ancient day it cost nearly a million dollars. Fires were lighted in the top of it and could be seen for miles out at sea. It was destroyed by an earthquake in the thirteenth century, but remains of it were visible until A.D.

1350. Being the tallest of all the Wonders, it: was naturally assigned to Saturn, the Father of the gods and the true illuminator of all humanity.

5. The Mausoleum at Halicarnassus was a magnificent monument erected by Queen Artemisia in memory of her dead husband, King Mausolus, from whose name the word *mausoleum* is derived. The designers of the building were Satyrus and Pythis, and four great sculptors were employed to ornament the edifice. The building, which was 114 feet long and 92 feet wide, was divided into five major sections (the senses) and surmounted by a pyramid (the spiritual nature of man). The pyramid rose in 24 steps (a sacred number), and upon the apex was a statue of King Mausolus in a chariot. His figure was 9 feet 9½ inches tall. Many attempts have been made to reconstruct the monument, which. was destroyed by an earthquake, but none has been altogether successful. This monument was sacred to the planet Mars and was built by an initiate for the enlightenment of the world.

6. The Gardens of Semiramis at Babylon--more commonly known as the Hanging Gardens--stood within the palace grounds of Nebuchadnezzar, near the Euphrates River. They rose in a terrace-like pyramid and on the top was a reservoir for the watering of the gardens. They were built about 600 B.C., but the name of the landscape artist has not been preserved. They symbolized the planes of the invisible world, and were consecrated to Venus as the goddess of love and beauty.

7. The Great Pyramid was supreme among the temples of the Mysteries. In order to be true to its astronomical symbolism, it must have been constructed about 70,000 years ago. It was the tomb of Osiris, and was believed to have been

built by the gods themselves, and the architect may have been the immortal Hermes. It is the monument of Mercury, the messenger of the gods, and the universal symbol of wisdom and letters.

www.ingramcontent.com/pod-product-compliance
Lightning Source LLC
LaVergne TN
LVHW041503070426
835507LV00009B/789